Distance Between

Distance Between
Copyright © 2018 Stacia Leigh
All rights reserved.

This is a work of fiction. Names, characters, places, and incidents are products of the author's imagination or are used fictitiously and are not to be construed as real. Any resemblance to actual events, locales, organizations, or persons, living or dead, is entirely coincidental.

The excerpts from *Dealing with Blue* and *Burnout,* originally titled *Riding with the Hides of Hell*, the cover design, photography, stories, and art are by Stacia Leigh at www.espialdesign.com.

No part of this book may be reproduced or distributed in any printed or electronic form without prior written permission by Stacia Leigh, except in the case of brief quotations embodied in reviews.

Please purchase only authorized editions and discourage piracy of copyrighted materials. Help support independent authors and artists!

ISBN-13: 978-1-7321435-4-8

ALSO BY STACIA LEIGH

♥

Dealing with Blue

Burnout

Hanging Around for You

*Sounds Complicated:
Blackout Poetry and Art*

To Ricco and Christine for making the
Bulgarian experience possible.
The trip opened up a well
of inspiration.

♥

Distance Between

Blackout Poetry and Art

by
Stacia Leigh

CLOUD NINE

Struggling to hold
a happy smile
on cloud nine.

want a kitten with a pink dress and pink eyes, and I'll name her Oopsie Loo. Isn't that cute?"

Marsha looked slightly rattled by the request as Mom engulfed Oopsie in her arms and pulled her back into an I-love-you-but-zip-it hug. J.J. knew Marsha had a hard time letting things go, so giving Suzy a doll she'd made was a pretty big deal.

Suzy held out her palm, and Marsha grabbed it with a trembling hand. Her blue eyes were lit up with unshed tears, and J.J. could tell Marsha was struggling to hold back a massive flood. J.J. looked away. God, he was getting choked up here.

"Now, let me get a picture of you two." Marsha cleared her throat and tapped on her phone screen. "I'll send it to your dad. He'll want to see his daughter looking so beautiful a happy. Smile!"

***

"Smile, smile, smile!" everyone said, holding up their camera phones, and Suzy smiled. In fact, she couldn't un-smile. She sat on cloud nine attached elbow to elbow with her Mr. Cool. God, she was floating.

Then, everyone said, "Goodbye, goodbye, goodbye! Have fun, drive safe, be good!" Suzy laughed, and like she was a helium balloon, J.J. tugged her out the front door. He kept tugging until he stopped at the chrome grill of his truck. He turned and faced her. Where was his

CROW'S FEET

I remember you put a smile on my face.
Now, I got the crow's feet.

Stacia Leigh

"I remember you **put a smile on my** **face.** **Now, I go** **the crow's feet**

crow's Feet by Stacia Leigh 6/6/18

TEAPOT

You stored feelings in a teapot,
but there was no room for me.

Stacia Leigh

"So are those boxes you stored in my closet more important than me and my feelings?"

"What about my feelings? Why can't I be happy, Suzette?" Marsha clenched her fist and held it over her heart. "Why do I have to keep giving in to you and Nick? Neither of you care about me."

"Oh, please. You're my mother, but you've never acted like one. All you care about is collecting fabric, old books, and teapots you never use."

"You're a selfish—you just want things your way."

"How can you expect me to live here…in this?" Suzy waved her hand at the hallway. "I worry every day about being trapped in here. Stuck." Suzy clapped a hand over her mouth to control her runaway emotions. "God, Mom, you don't get it. You surround yourself with this crap, and it means more to you than living in a clean, safe place. And what about your health? I mean, rats are dirty. They carry diseases."

"This place may be cluttered, but it's safe, Suzette."

"No, it's not. Not when there're dead rats in our kitchen."

"Oh, man," J.J. whispered, wiping a hand up his forehead to clutch his hair.

"J.J." Gary said firmly and jerked his head toward the door.

"It's not safe. And what about me?" Suzy jabbed a finger against her own chest. "Your own flesh and blood, your own daughter. I'm your only kid, but I've always had to live with dad because there was no room for me

Teapot by Stacia Leigh 2/7/2017

A HUNDRED TIMES

A hundred times I'd let us be wrong.
Remember?
A hundred times you agreed
to spend as little time as possible at home.

Stacia Leigh

> a hundred times
>
> I'd let you drive us, you'd be wrong
>
> remember?
>
> hundred times
>
> you agreed
>
> to spend as little time as possible at home

A Hundred Times by Stacia Leigh   6.29.17

ON ALERT

The princess searched the court
for teeth and red eyes.
She couldn't risk her neck again.

Dealing with Blue

peered through the smudged glass into a dark room. No Suzy.

The princess was on the run.

Where was she? What was she doing? He turned and searched over his shoulder toward the Badger Court sign, the direction of Main Street. She could have gone to Grubby's for an early dinner or to Butterhorn or to the mall. He raked his teeth over his raw lip, relishing the tinge of pain before turning to the right, toward the lake and the meadow. He saw red as in red, coppery hair pulled back in a slick ponytail. Suzy popped into view a trailer house down, but when she lifted her eyes to him, she stopped.

Last time J.J. talked to her, he stood below this same window and things didn't go so well. He suction-cupped his palm onto the glass pane and shifted it to the side, wide open—all the while watching her watching him. Oh, they were going to talk aright and on equal footing. J.J. couldn't risk her slamming his face in the window, not to mention any more fingers. He had to make things right. He just had to.

"J.J.!" Suzy started to run. "No!"

"I came to talk!" He hollered over his shoulder. Keeping his neck positioned just right and the weight off his splint, he jumped up and tilted forward. He bounced once on his fat lip—Ow!—and bounced again, swinging his legs around in front of him. Smartest move? Probably not. A zip of pain climbed up his neck to the back of his

ON ALERT BY
STACIA-LEIGH
2/7/2017

241

SHE MAY BE CRAZY

Eyes held her gaze,
a dangerous mistake.
She may be crazy.

Dealing with Blue

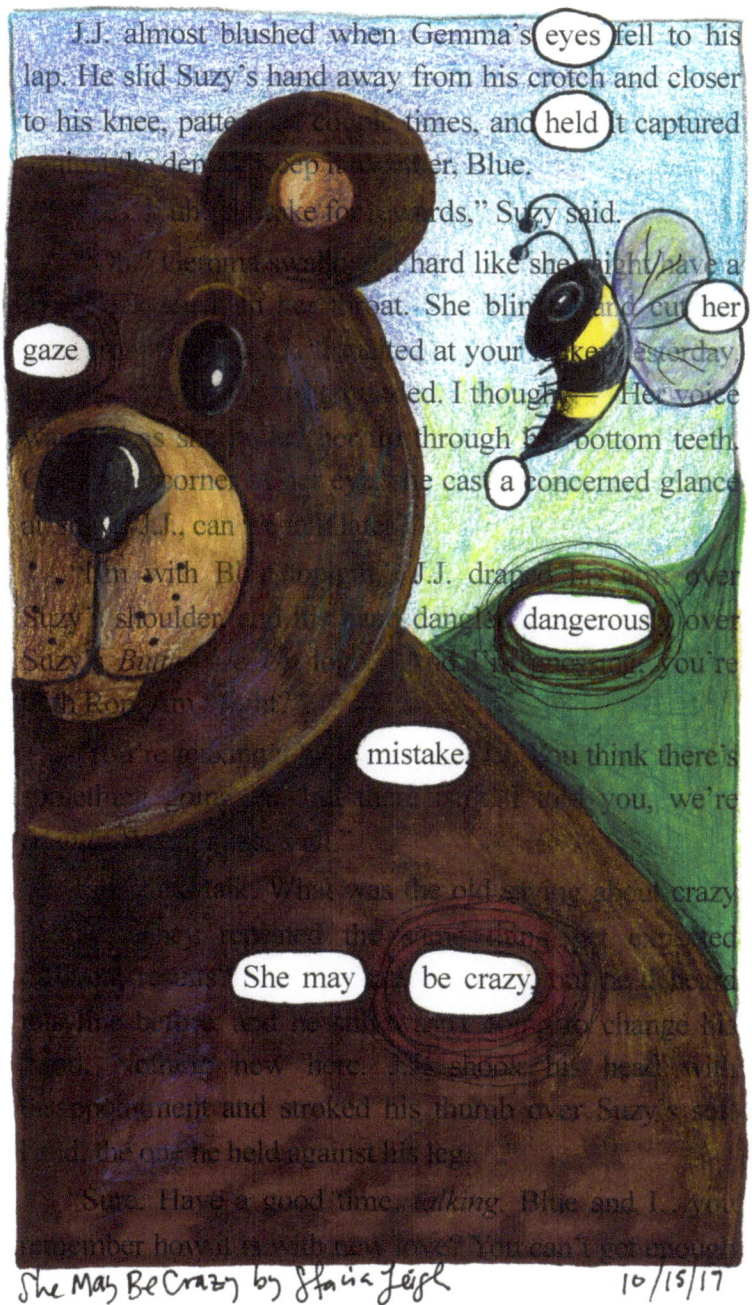

She May Be Crazy by Stacie Leigh   10/15/17

DEEP ROOT 2

A strong connection was a deep root,
all tangled inside.

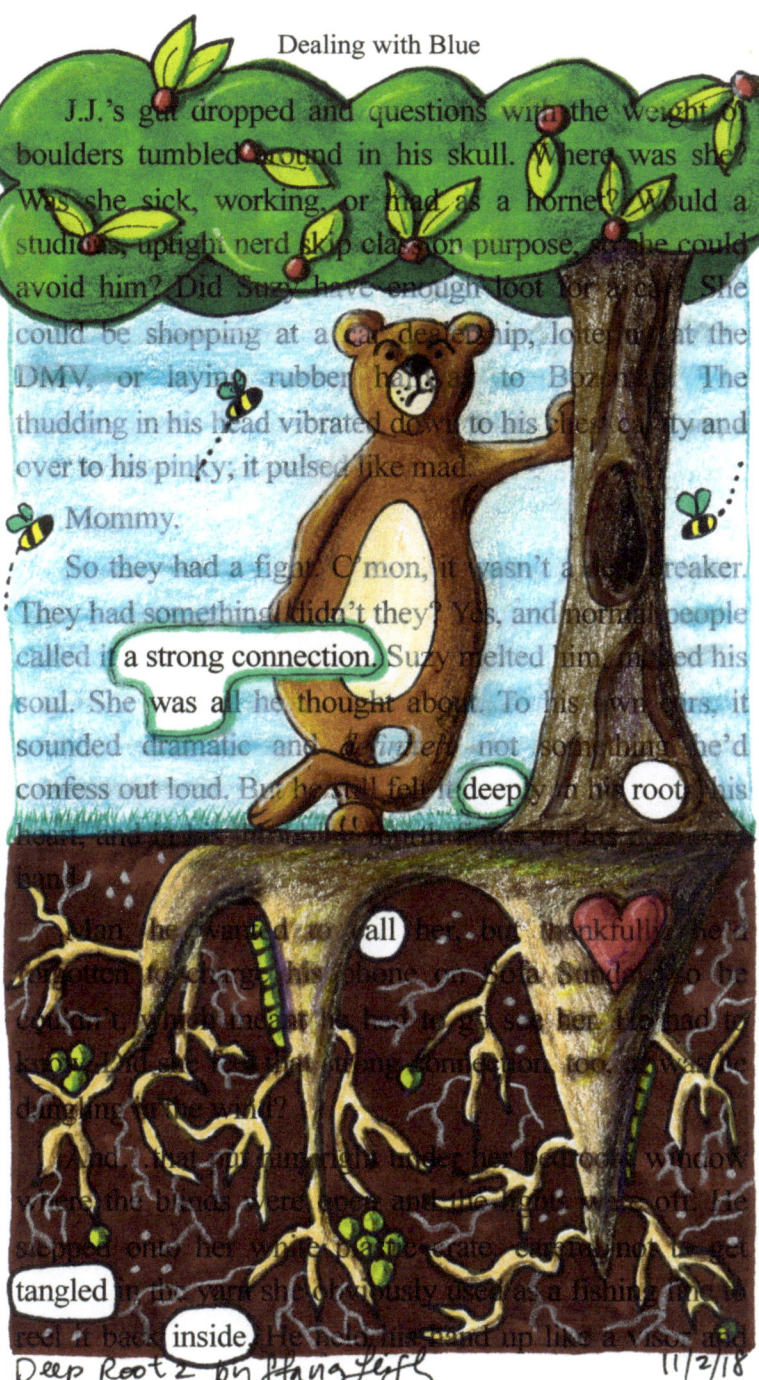

BLURRED LINES

He couldn't appreciate the right moment.
The lines blurred.

Dealing with Blue

watching him from under her thick black eyelashes. She waited while a hefty mom and pop couple lumbered past.

"What are you doing with her, J.J.?" Gemma asked casually, but her long denim leg rocked back and forth with a nervous edge.

"Good question. If he wanted Gemma back, though, he couldn't tell her the truth, could he? He opened his mouth, but the right words wouldn't come. How could he tell Gemma about Suzy? Would Gemma appreciate how Suzy mystified him with her quiet and subdued nature? She was captivating and enticing even while she hid behind those nerdy, dark-rimmed glasses. And the turquoise tab on the zipper of her jacket, the one snugged up tight under her chin. He was supposed to want to slowly pull that thing down, right?

What was it about Suzy's aqua-blue eyes? Or was it her mermaid hair, loose and free one moment, then wrestled up tight and controlled the next? He liked her curves on top, the dip in her waist, out and down over her cushion. He shook his head. Why was he thinking about Suzy's body right now? The lines between him and his pretend girlfriend blurred like he was looking through water. But there was something there, trying to take shape.

So...no. He couldn't say anything at all.

Gemma's lips turned up into a smile, and she pushed off the wall to drape her arms over his shoulders.

BLUEBIRD

Love, which stretched her chest,
had turned restrained.

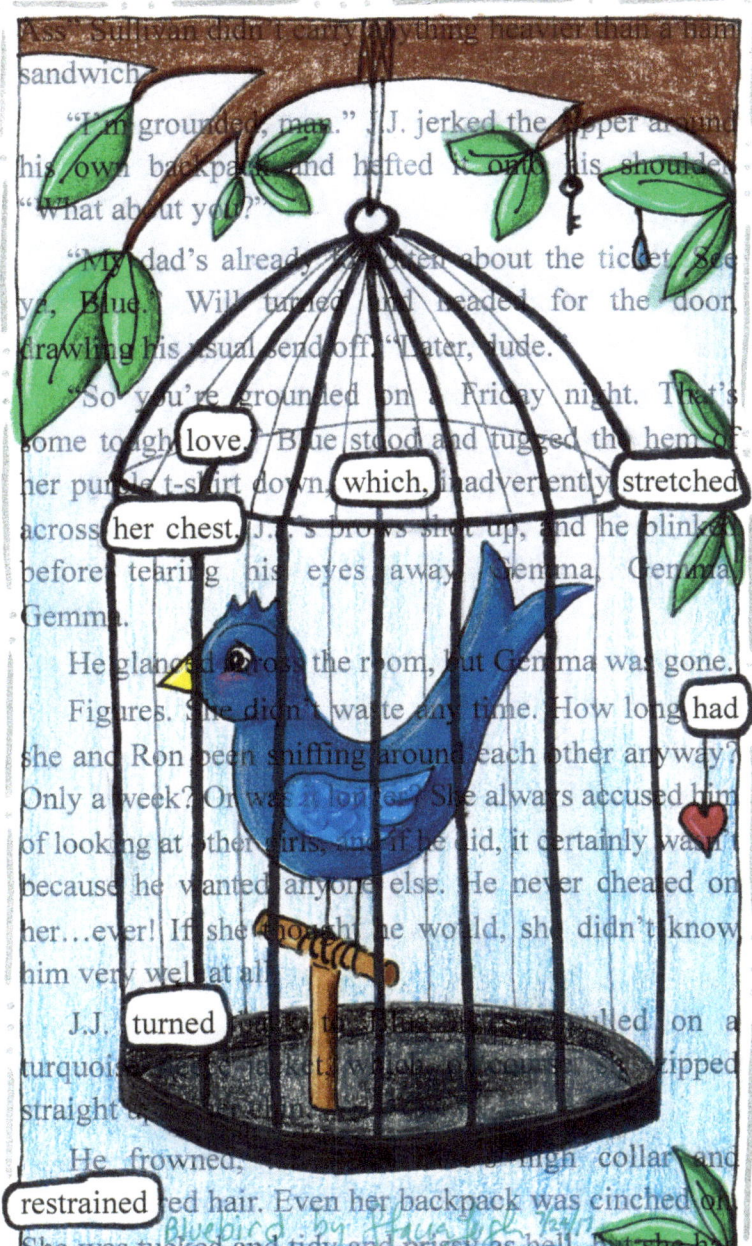

WORRIES

When all was dark
worries could get back in
and last 4ever.

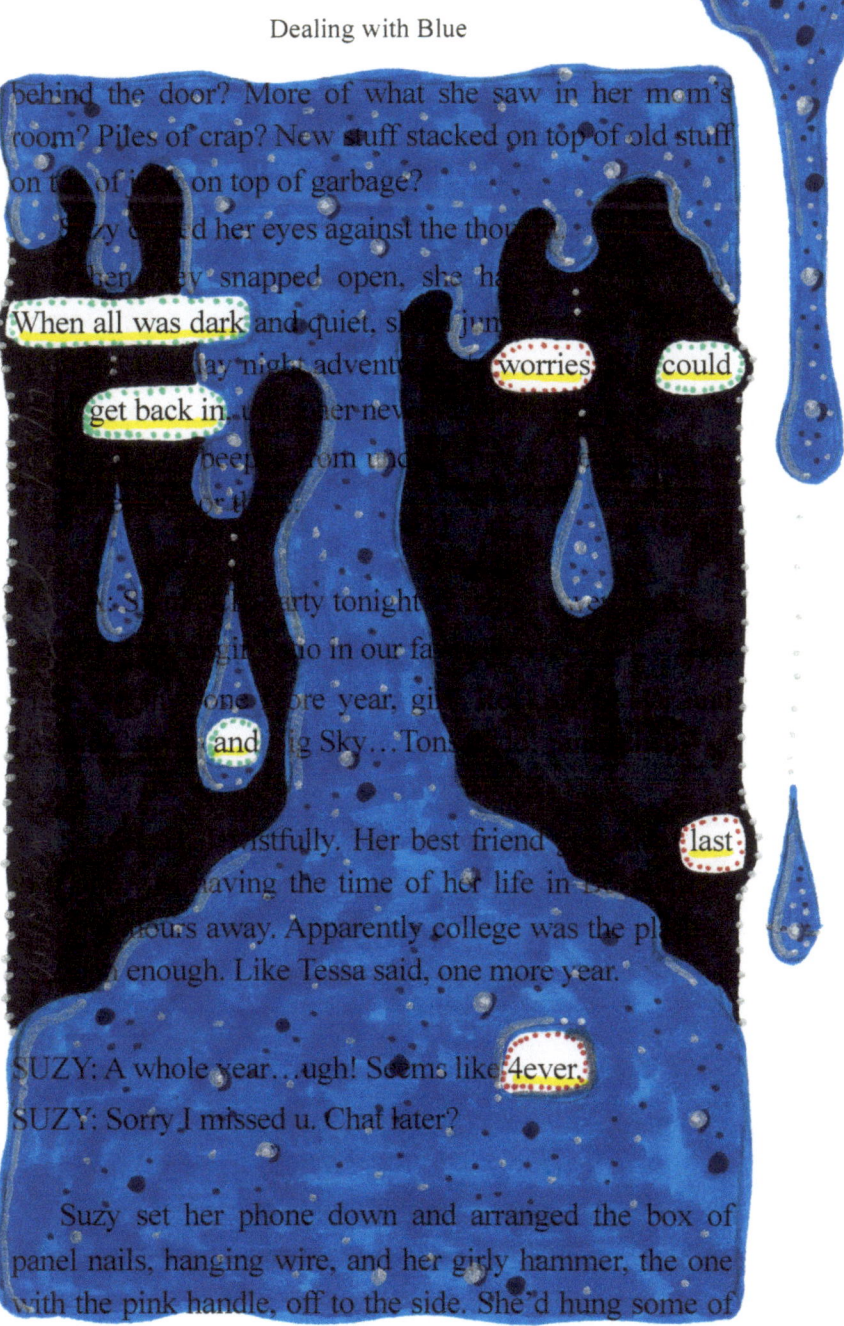

When all was dark • get back in • worries • could • and • last • 4ever

THE RAIN

The rain rolled down her cheek
and fell into a dream.

Dealing with Blue

their hands. Would J.J. even look at her, or was she easily forgotten?

There was no more *What if?* and no more *Why not?* Pathetic.

The cream bath towel barricading the one-inch gap under her bedroom door hadn't moved, a good sign. She clutched J.J.'s skinny flashlight from her fleece pocket and rolled off the mattress to kneel on the carpet. She swept the light beam back-and-forth under her bed with a triple-check in each corner. No rats.

Suzy shoved the flashlight back into her pocket and climbed onto her covers, her knees tucked under her chin. She couldn't stop thinking about J.J. and Gemma. Would he remember the things he'd told her when they were caught in the rain? Their casual relationship hadn't even lasted thirty-two hours. Her comic heart cracked open a little more and a fat tear rolled down her cheek, then another. She squeezed the pillow to her face and let them fall, fast and furious. After a long, damp pity party, she slumped like a boneless cracker and fell into a dreamless sleep.

Rap, rap, rap!

Suzy jerked awake and blinked. Oh, God! That had to be J.J. She straightened and chased any smudges off her face with the heel of her palm, then glanced at the time on her phone. It was late… very late. She should have turned

THE RAIN BY Hana Leigh   3/16/17

225

PROTECTIVE HOUSE

The house said,
"I'm afraid I can't leave you
alone with this storm."

Stacia Leigh

Protective House by Stacia Leigh   8/5/17

HERE IT LIES

Freedom died on the paper.
All of it.

Stacia Leigh

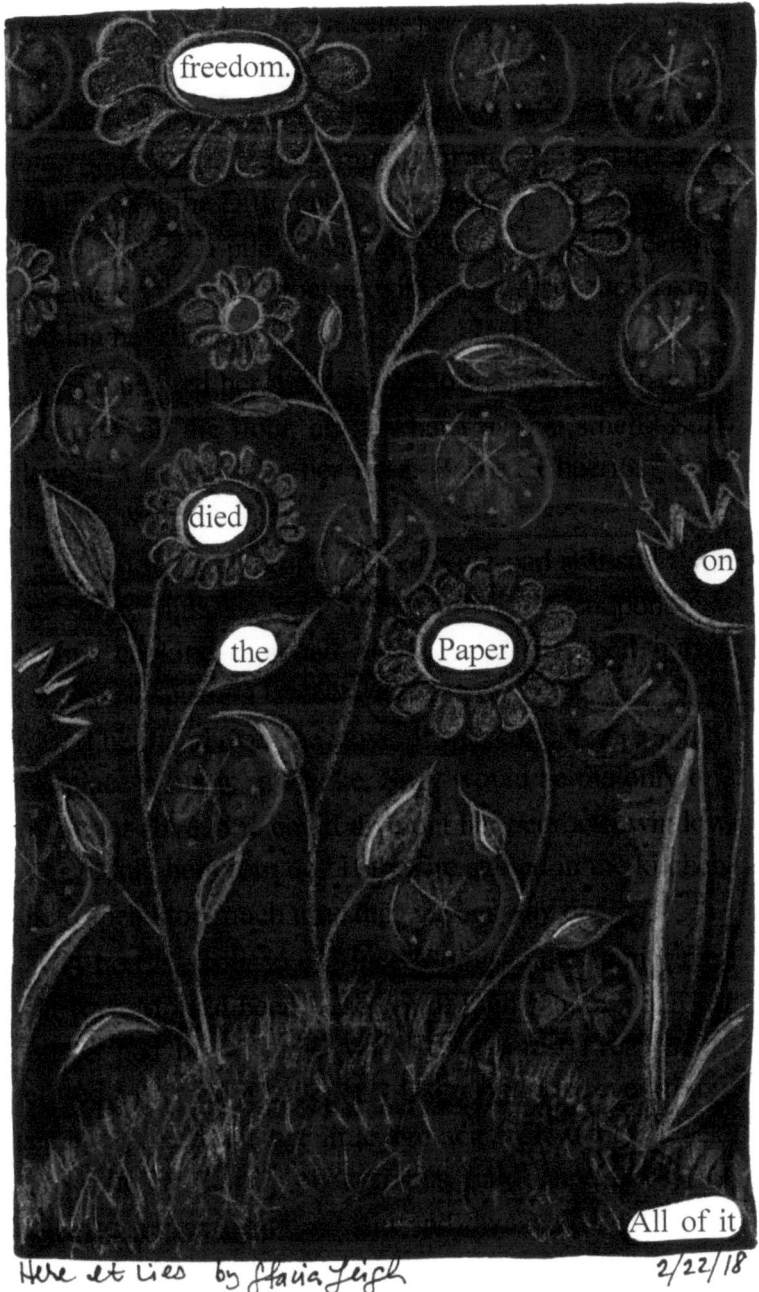

Here it lies by Stacia Leigh   2/22/18

FREEDOM

Freedom from control freaks
wouldn't be so bad.

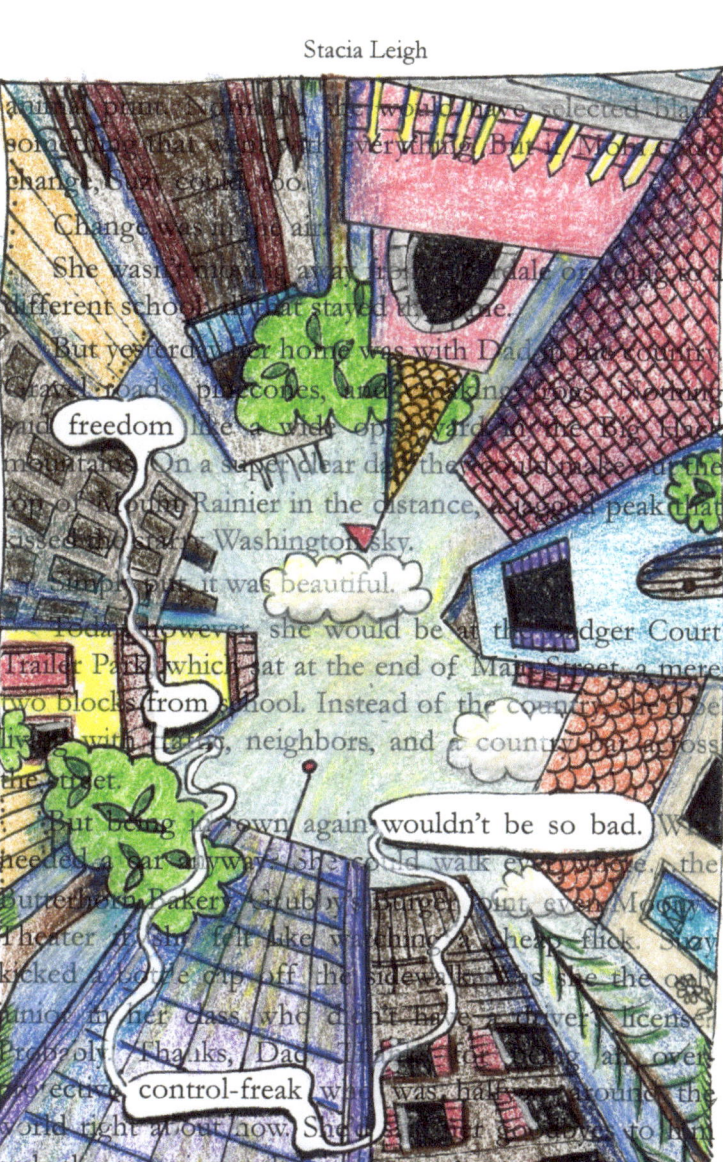

WON'T STICK

Something bitter in you
won't stick.

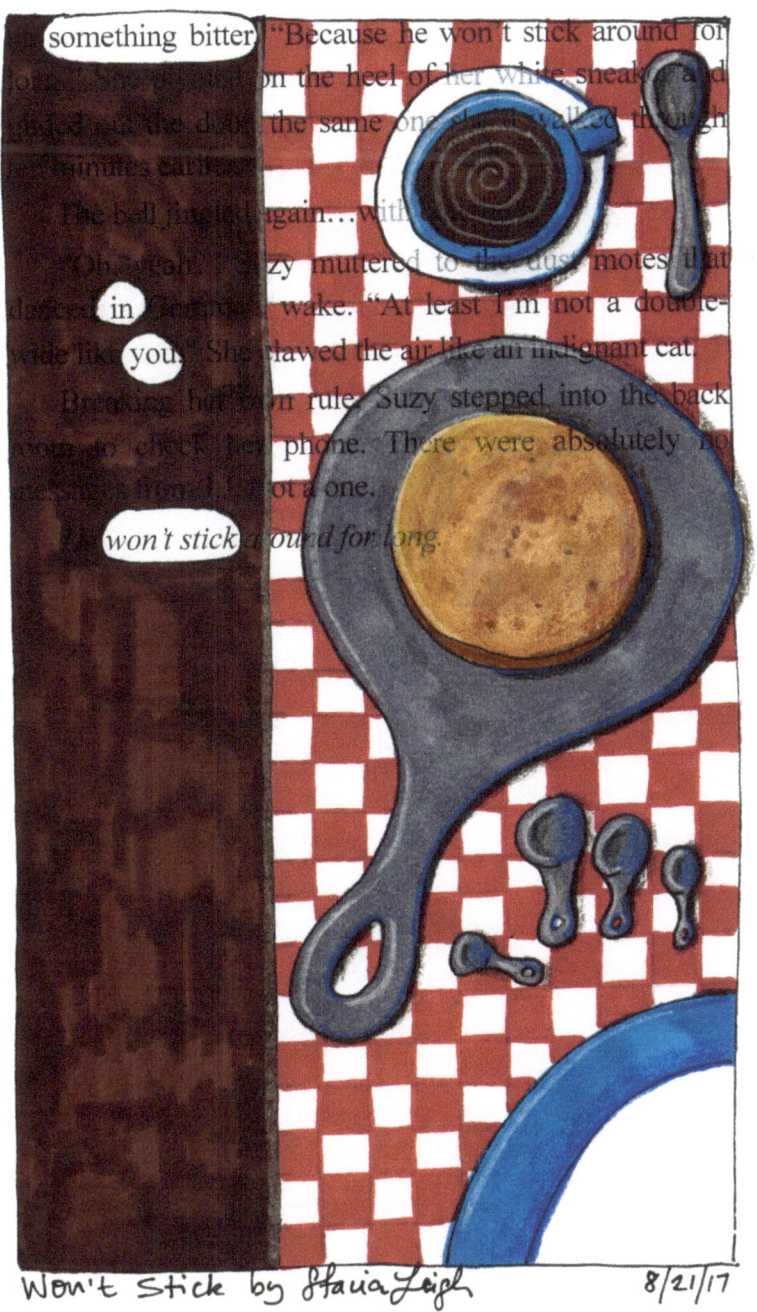

Won't Stick by Stacia Leigh   8/21/17

NEW BEGINNINGS

It was time to begin,
to stop all the crying and go.

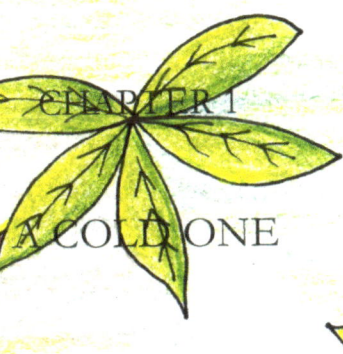

Riding with the Hides of Hell

CHAPTER 1

A COLD ONE

Whenever Will heard his mom's brusque voice in his head, it was time to crack open a cold one.

Will, this is your mom speaking.

Like now.

Eleven months after she'd been killed, and in the beginning, he'd cried oceans of tears. His joints ached from dehydration. But it didn't take him long to discover the beauty of getting drunk and passing out. Beer was mostly water; it was hydrating, right? Water that buzzed his brain, so he could stop all the crying and go unconscious through the night. It was sort of like sleeping, but better, because his mind turned into a vacant tube with no dreams and no voices.

When he wasn't drunk—or drunk enough—she'd sneak up on him and interrupt his thoughts in the same way. *Will, Will, Will. This is your mother speaking, speaking, speaking.*

It was like his mom sat on the cushion of his brain with a bull horn. Her tone rang out crisp and clear, like the good old days when she'd harp at him to load the dishwasher or to ask for the loaf pan from the top shelf. He'd gripe about it, and she'd tell him to be thankful he

New Beginnings by Stacia Leigh 1/16/18

BREAK OUT

Break out of the pothole,
and picture a heart in your mind.

Stacia Leigh

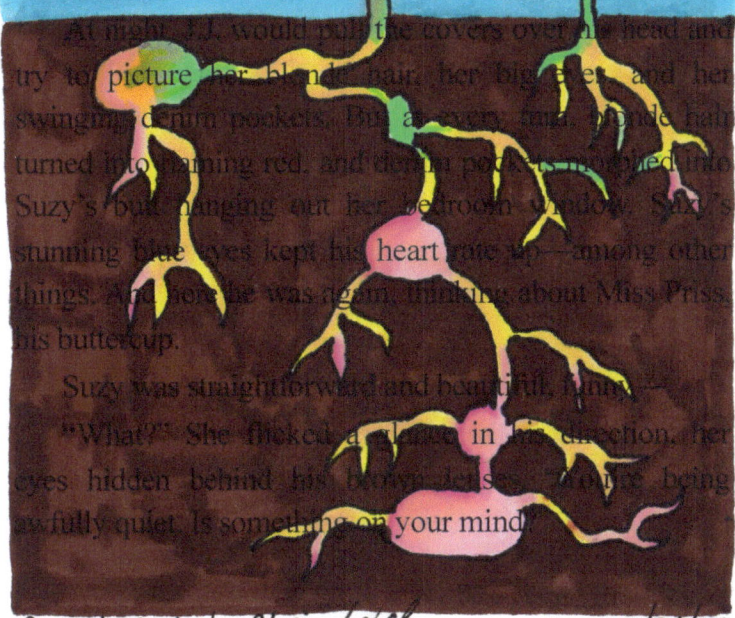

Break Out by Stacia Leigh   2/24/17

START AGAIN

Perched on the edge is an epic start.
Just dive in at the beginning.

Stacia Leigh

→ perched on the edge

an epic

start

just dive in, at the beginning.

Start Again by Stacia Leigh   9/2/2018

CAN AND WILL

This time, there was no other reality.

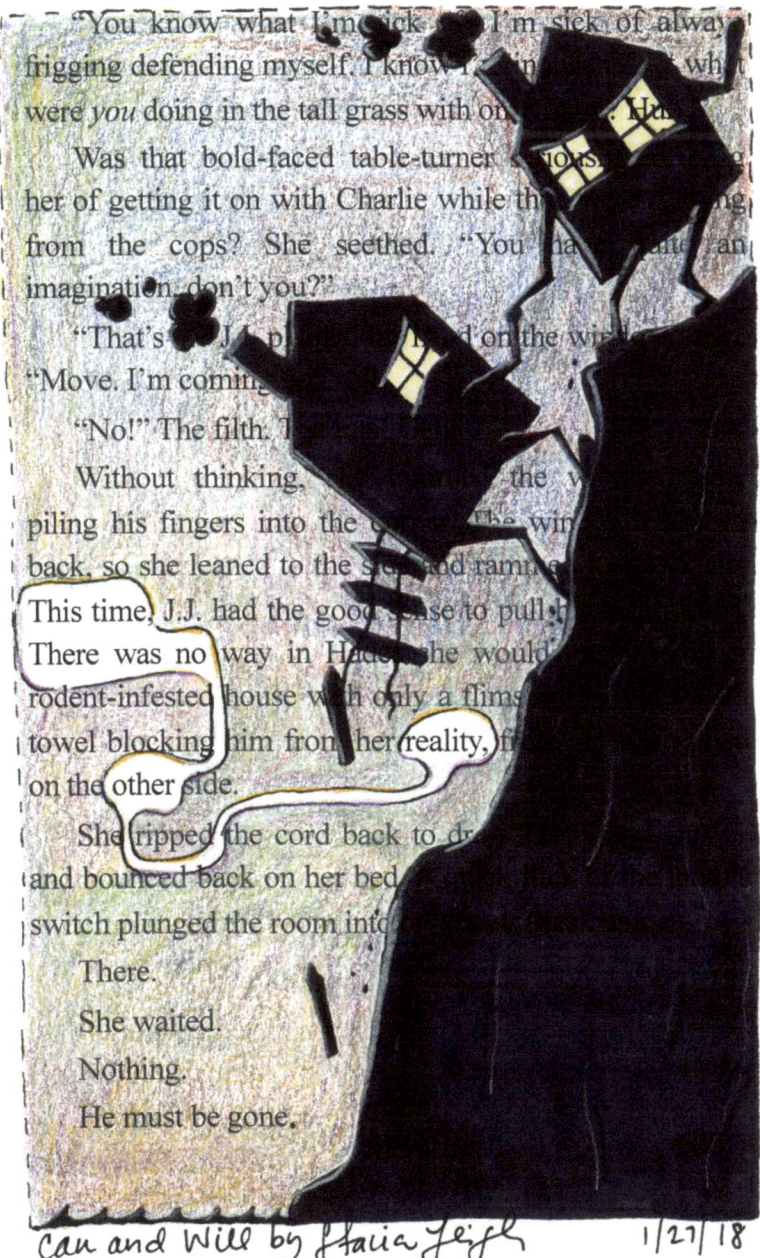

SEA OF VERVE

Step into the Sea of Verve
before you go.

Dealing with Blue

did have a moral obligation to make sure things stayed contained. She didn't need a wildfire on her hands.

She cursed under her breath and trudged along the perimeter next to the wallflowers, scanning for a way to break into the pulsing crowd. Charlie, her best student, slouched next to a row of wide-eyed girls in pretty dresses. His gaze was on Suzy, but according to their personality tests, those two wouldn't have been a good match. They were too similar. Opposites attracted. Didn't he know that from class? Mrs. Norton shook her head. Surely, she'd mentioned it.

She stepped into the sea of elbows, knee caps, hips, and hair and wove through the fray, holding her arms out to keep the gangly feet off her new Pompadour heels. She lost her target in the crowd and stopped, only to be jostled from behind. It was Ron, rocking back and forth like a stiff plank while clutching at Gemma's sequined waist. The poor dear had misery painted all over her face, eyes numbly glued on a pair of slow dancers.

Aha! J.J. and Suzy, the igniting duo.

She eased past Ron and clicked her heels to an abrupt stop beside Mr. Radborne. Whoever thought slow music at a prom was a good idea? Teen verve, anyone hear of it? She took in his freshly shorn hairdo before formally tapping his shoulder.

"Why don't you two cool down and go get a drink?" Mrs. Norton's lips turned up into a smile at their puzzled

299

COURAGE

My life vest is in the boat,
and I'm in the water.

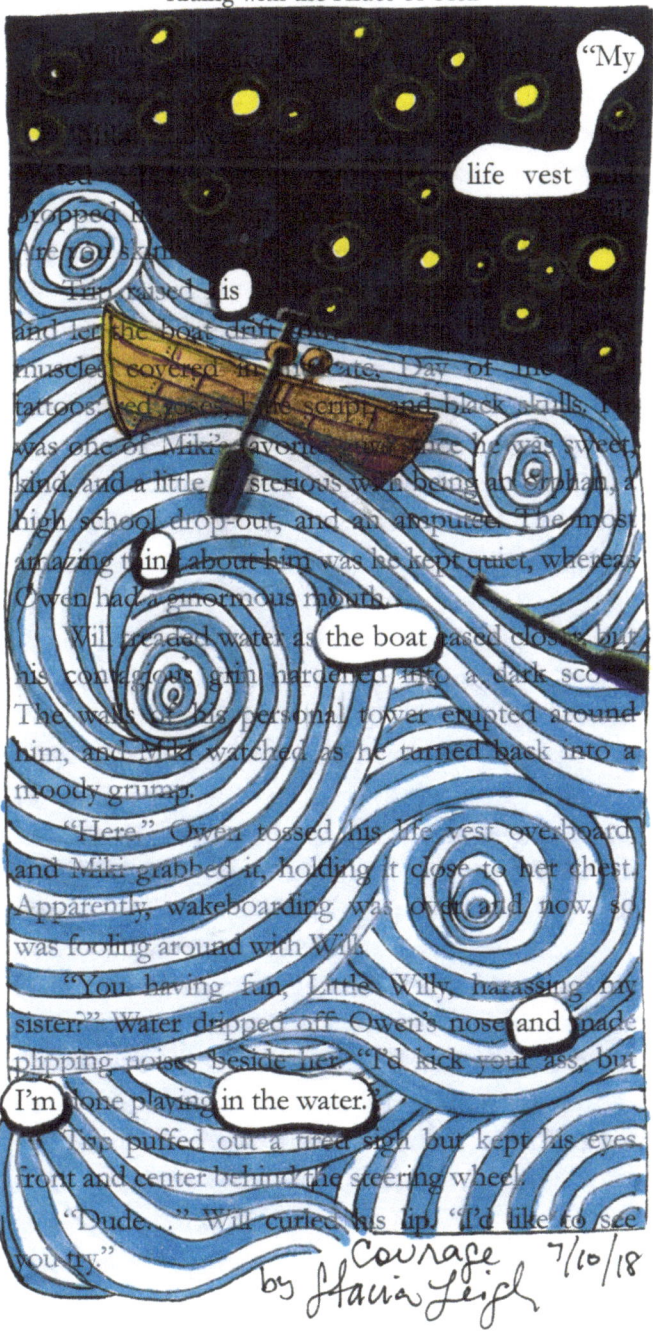

SIGN IN THE ROAD

The universe was busy thinking about
one more sign in the road.

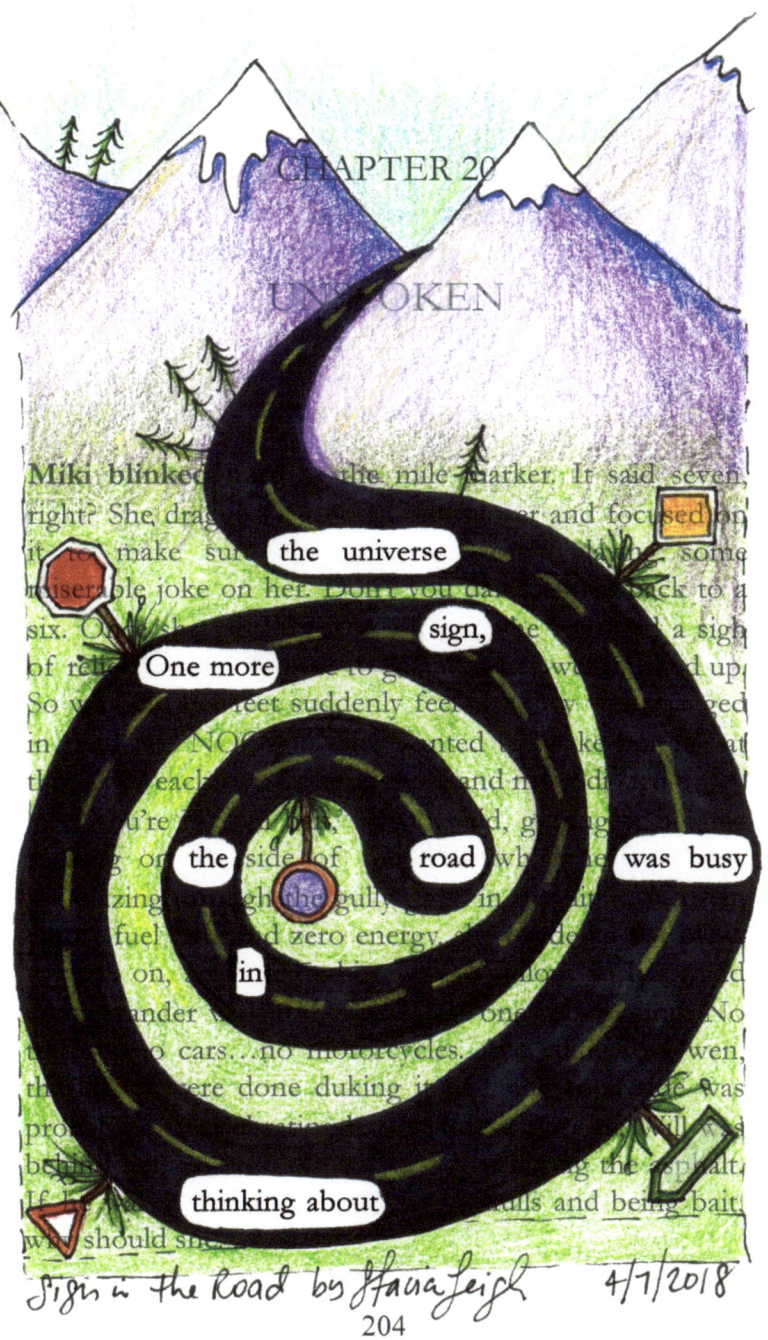

HOME ON THE ROAD

Heaven was putting distance
between her and everyone.

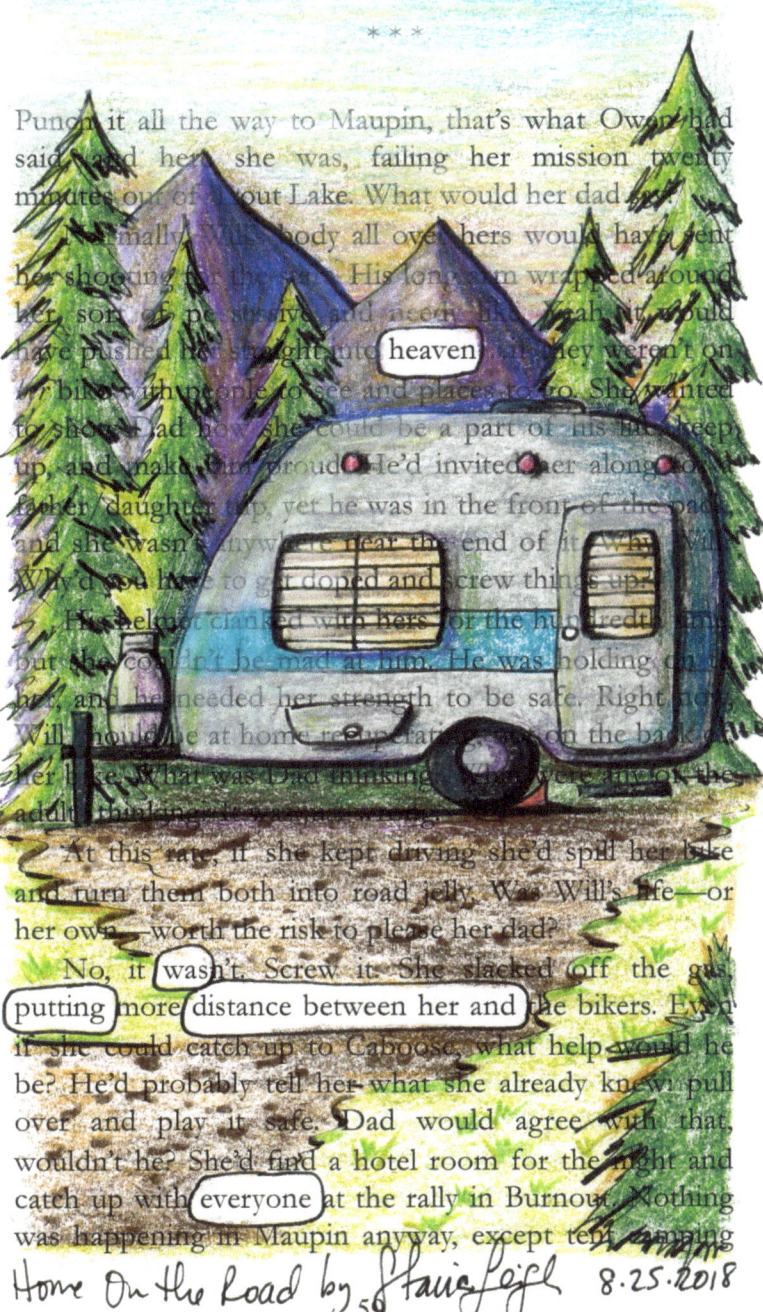

heaven

putting more distance between her and

everyone

Home On the Road by Stacie Leigh 8.25.2018

BACKWARD AND FORWARD

    Remember to forget.
    Forget to remember.

Riding with the Hides of Hell

because J.J. got it. He understood that if the tables were turned, Will would have his back. That's what friends were for.

"The drop-off went smooth. He called in, said he had a tail, and we haven't heard from him since." Leo's words drifted by. "And coincidentally a couple P's were seen milling around here. I'm getting a bad vibe. Not good."

Will opened his eyes and studied the air vent on the dash while he focused on what the guys were saying. Who hadn't they heard from? Who were they talking about? P's was short for P-Scum or P-Skulls, all nicknames for the rival club, the Pulver Skulls.

It took a while before Uncle Shorty acknowledged that he heard Leo. Then he said, "Anything else?"

"So what're we gonna do?" another voice murmured.

"Not here." Leo's voice rumbled. "But I'm looking at an earlier departure."

"Agreed," Uncle Shorty said. "I'll get my side together and you—"

"Yup. I'll do the same." Leo cut in. "We'll meet later."

Will strained to hear the grunts of acceptance followed by a cryptic discussion on preferred hardware, women and who was going to the rally.

The rally. Will closed his eyes again. He didn't want to go. He'd have to ride on the back of someone else's bike like an old lady. God, he'd never hear the end of it. What's more, they expected him to let go of his mom's ashes, her last slice of apple pie, and he'd have to quit drinking. They'd make him remember what he wanted to forget, and make him forget what he wanted to remember, and he didn't want any part of it. What he did want was to be left alone.

Backward & Forward by Stacia Leigh   1/21/18

37

DON'T WAIT

Don't wait for me.
I'm ready to survive without you.

Dealing with Blue

of sheep, until they pushed through the double doors to the outside.

"Hey! I'm not a doll, okay?" Suzy yelled at the back of his head, trying to pull her hand free, put the skids on, and keep on her feet, all at the same time. "I'm in charge of my body, and I don't appreciate—"

"Sorry." J.J. slowed, letting her hand go to rake his hair back. "Gemma was waiting for me, and with Will… never mind. I just wanted to get out of there. I didn't want to talk to either of 'em anyway."

"I thought that was the whole point? She gets jealous, wants you back, and we break up. Right?"

"I don't know," he said.

"You don't know?"

"Uh…I mean the timing." He rubbed his neck. "I wasn't feeling it. I'm not ready."

"Timing…what? What does that have to do with her pleading for your undying affections?" Suzy cupped her cheeks and batted her eyelashes while cranking out some southern belle. "Oh, J.J., how can I survive without you? My sweet, sweet—" She dropped her hands and stepped out of character mode. "What does J.J. stand for anyway?"

"James Jefferson." He calmly folded his arms across his chest and watched her.

"Oh, James," Suzy said breathlessly. Who knew she had such a knack for impersonations? She would've nailed it, if Gemma were from the deep south. "I'm sorry I'm such a vile twit with no real intelligence. Please…"

165

50

STACIA LEIGH

…grew up in the Flathead Valley and is a graduate of Montana State University. She currently resides in the state of Washington with a couple of cherrier rescue mutts, two arty farties, and a computer nerd.

Burnout is a 2016 PNWA Literary Contest finalist for young adult. Stacia's first independently published novel, *Dealing with Blue,* is a 2015 PNWA Literary Contest finalist for young adult as well as a 2016 Nancy Pearl Book Award finalist.

She enjoys writing what she loves to read, a flirty romance that's light on the angst and heavy on the fun.

Want to learn more about Stacia's upcoming books and latest projects or just want to swing by for a quick hello? Boom! Done. All you have to do is visit her here:

www.stacialeigh.com

* * *

MY NERD SELF

My nerd self
enjoys a "heavy" book.

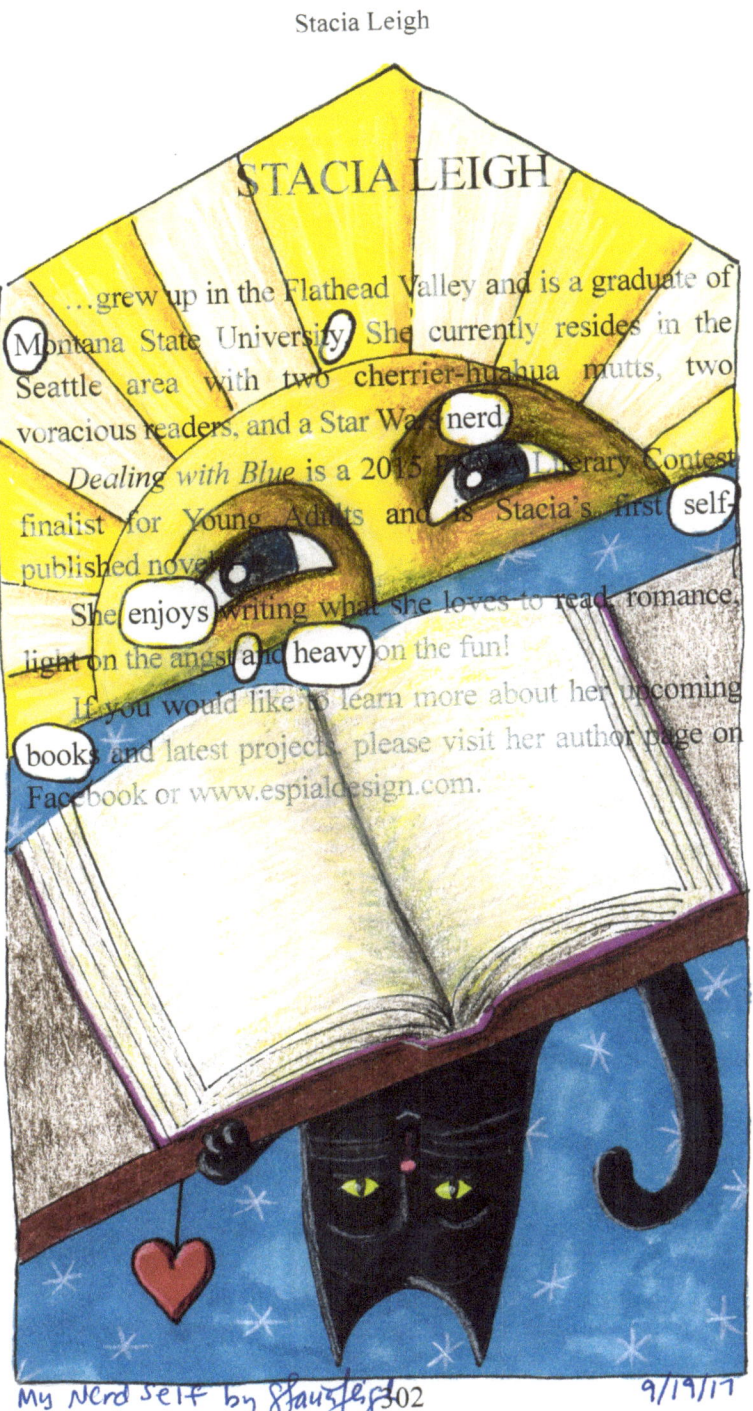

Behind the blackout poems and doodle art are two young adult love stories with flirt, grit and small town fun. Don't miss out!

Dealing
with Blue
by
Stacia Leigh

"Name your price, Suzy Blue. Everyone's got one."— Life used to be normal until Suzy Blue moves into the trailer park with her mom. Then things turn secretive and claustrophobic. To get out of the house, Suzy accepts a deal with the charming neighbor boy, J.J. Radborne. All he needs is a pretend girlfriend for bonfires, fun, and a possible prom date, and all she needs is driving lessons to get out of this town...for good.

"You're making a huge mistake, J.J."— So says Gemma, J.J.'s ex-girlfriend. She's turning up the heat in a confusing mind game, and J.J. knows exactly who to team up with: Suzy Blue. She's cute, convenient, and even sorta funny. More importantly, Gemma's already jealous. Hey, she started it; he's just playing along. So, yeah. Suzy...perfect. Now, if she'd only cooperate.

Dealing with Blue is a small town love story set in the Pacific Northwest. It's about a strong girl and a bad boy peeling back the layers to discover what's true.

FINALIST 2015 PNWA Literary Contest for Young Adults
FINALIST 2016 PNWA Nancy Pearl Book Award

ISBN: 978-0692608814

Burnout
by
Stacia Leigh

"I have a plan."— Miki Holtz isn't some rebellious sixteen-year-old just because she dyed her hair blue and rides a motorcycle. She's an independent girl who knows what, when, and how to get things done… almost. She can't seem to gain her dad's attention or make a connection with her soul crush, Will Sullivan. But when her dad invites her along to the Burnout Biker Rally—and Will is going, too—she jumps at the chance to turn her luck around.

"I don't like the way you like me."— While grieving the death of his mom, Will Sullivan has turned into an undeniable couch potato until he's forced on a road trip with his dad's motorcycle buddies as some kind of biker therapy. What's worse? He's paired up with the prez's daughter, Miki, a girl who once humiliated him in front of his friends—a girl he can't forgive…or forget.

Burnout is an adventure story set in the Pacific Northwest where a strong girl and a moody boy discover love while trying to survive on a road trip from hell.

FINALIST for Young Adult in the 2016 PNWA Literary Contest under the title *Riding with the Hides of Hell*.

ISBN: 978-1732143500

www.ingramcontent.com/pod-product-compliance
Lightning Source LLC
Chambersburg PA
CBHW040238220526
45473CB00001B/294